RESUMÉS
FOR FREELANCERS

*Make Your Resumé
an Effective Marketing Tool
. . . and More*

SHEILA BUFF & RUTH E. THALER-CARTER

THE-EFA.ORG

Previously published by the EFA as *Résumés for Freelancers — How to Turn Your Traditional Résumé into an Effective Marketing Tool* by Sheila Buff (2007).

266 West 37ᵗʰ St. 20ᵗʰ Floor
New York, NY 10018
office@the-efa.org

Sheila Buff & Ruth E. Thaler-Carter, *Resumés for Freelancers: Make Your Resumé an Effective Marketing Tool . . . and More*

ISBN paperback   978-1-880407-15-8
ISBN ebook   978-1-880407-16-5

Published in the United States of America by the Editorial Freelancers Association.
Subject Categories: **LANGUAGE ARTS & DISCIPLINES** / Publishers & Publishing Industry | Writing / Business Aspects | **BUSINESS & ECONOMICS** / Careers / Resumes | Job Hunting

Legal Disclaimer
While the publisher and author have made every attempt to verify that the information provided in this book is correct and up to date, the publisher and author assume no responsibility for any error, inaccuracy, or omission.

The advice, examples, and strategies contained herein are not suitable for every situation. Neither the publisher nor author shall be liable for damages arising therefrom. This book is not intended for use as a source of legal or financial advice. Running a business involves complex legal and financial issues. You should always retain competent legal and financial professionals to provide guidance.

EFA Publications Director: Robin Martin
Copyeditor: Molly McCowen and Marcia Ford
Proofreader: Amy Spungen
Book Designer: Kevin Callahan | BNGO Books
Cover Designer: Ann Marie Manca

Contents

List of Figures

Introduction

One important element of being a freelancer is showing potential clients what you've done in the past in a way that highlights what you can do for them. Prospective clients may ask you for your resumé to help evaluate your skills. You also might send unsolicited resumés to clients you hope to work for. Either way, an effective resumé can be one of your best marketing tools.

Unfortunately, even a good resumé that documents your past jobs in the industry and is clearly written, attractively designed, and written in accordance with advice from the best job-hunting books may not generate positive results as often as you'd like. Why not?

The problem may be that you're applying techniques for finding a full-time job to the search for freelance assignments. It's like using a rock instead of a hammer to drive in a nail: crude, clumsy, and effective just often enough that you'll try it again. As one colleague put it, a freelancer's resumé is different because all you want is a gig, not a permanent job—a date, not a marriage proposal.

In today's marketplace, you need alternatives to a traditional resumé, not just visually in terms of content or format, but to better suit social media and other online environments. In fact, for many freelancers, a formal resumé may no longer be necessary or of primary importance. A more efficient approach is to modify your resumé in order to turn it into the marketing tool you need.

Crafting a skills-based version, also known as a functional resumé, is a powerful exercise that can help you focus your mind on freelancing instead of staff employment. A skills-based resumé makes you think about how your training and experience have prepared you for freelancing, and how you present yourself to prospective clients on your website and through social media and marketing materials.

Traditional vs.
Functional Resumés

Traditional resumés work well for people looking for traditional jobs in traditional settings—that is, full-time, in-house positions. The traditional resumé includes your career summary, lists your work experience with employment dates and job titles in reverse chronological order, and concludes with information about your education. This type of resumé is an effective tool if you've progressed up a clearly defined career ladder, are looking for a job on the next rung, or want to enter or return to full-time, in-house employment.

For serious freelancers committed to self-employment, the traditional resumé is fundamentally flawed. If you've been freelancing for a while, it doesn't accommodate the variety of projects you've probably worked on as a freelancer. If the last full-time job you had was years ago, the reverse chronological approach makes it look like you've been unemployed since then. More importantly, a traditional resumé doesn't tell a potential client whether you can do the job. Managing editors looking for proofreaders, for instance, don't care what your previous job title was or where you went to college. They want to know that you'll do a good, fast, accurate job on schedule and on budget—in other words, that you are a skilled, reliable professional.

One of the best ways to present yourself as a dependable editorial professional is with a functional resumé. This type of resumé describes

Figure 1. Traditional resumé.

your skills, abilities, and accomplishments. It may mention previous job experience and educational attainments, but the focus is on your skills.

Although most clients don't realize it, a functional resumé is what they really want to see, because it tells them at a glance that you have the skills they need. To illustrate this point, compare the two versions of the resumé in Figures 1 and 2.

Figure 1 is in the familiar reverse chronological order. It's a good, solid resumé, attractively presented. It shows that the next step for this person is a higher editorial rung at a large trade magazine.

The human resources director and executive editor at a magazine will appreciate this resumé, but the managing editor of a college textbook division looking for a freelancer may discard it, for two reasons. First, according to this resumé, this is a magazine person, not a textbook person. Many editors tend to think in well-worn grooves. If the resumé

CHECKING IT TWICE

TERESA REILLY

599 Central Avenue | Middletown, NJ 07074 | 201-555-4321
Teresareilly@hmail.com | teresareilly.com | LinkedIn.com/in/teresareilly

SKILLS AND ABILITIES

Experienced magazine editor with outstanding layout and design skills.

EDITING

Extensive experience in book, newsletter, magazine, and website editing and copyediting using AP and CMOS style.
Skilled proofreader at all production levels, including pdfs and bluelines.

WRITING

News and feature writing for consumer and trade magazines and newsletters.
News and feature writing for magazine websites.
Writing press releases, brochures, and publicity materials.

DESIGN

Expert level skills in InDesign, Photoshop, PowerPoint, Autodesk Sketchbook Pro, digital photography.

SELECTED CLIENTS

Toy Weekly, Skylark Publishing
Modern Toys magazine, Adventure Publishing
Toyworld.com website
Parents magazine
Smart Lab Books
HarperOne Books

PRO BONO

Founding board member, Women in Toys
Member at large, Board of Governors, Editorial Freelancers Association

EDUCATION

University of Arizona, Tucson, B.A. Journalism, *magna cum laude*
Managing editor, *Arizona Daily Wildcat*, 2013–14
Smith Award for Outstanding Student Journalism, 2012

Figure 2. Functional resumé.

doesn't fit the groove, out it goes, without a glance to see if the skills used in the magazine jobs could be applied to textbooks. Second, even if the resumé was sent in response to an ad seeking freelancers, it describes someone who clearly is not a full-time freelancer; she's either freelancing on the side to make some extra money, or she's between jobs and will go back in-house as soon as a full-time position becomes available. In either case, the managing editor may not want to add the applicant to their roster of reliable full-time freelancers.

Now consider the functional resumé in Figure 2. Remember, this is the same person with the same skills, but those skills are presented in a way that's designed to get freelance assignments from busy, overworked editors.

Let's start at the top. Instead of just a name and address, there's a catchy business name. The managing editor knows at once that this is a resumé from a professional freelancer, and they may be more inclined to take the rest of the page seriously because of this. It lists the freelancer's skills by function—editing, for example. Within the skill, it lists the particular areas of expertise.

This functional resumé also lists clients by name, which is important and reassuring information for someone hiring a freelancer. It suggests that you've worked successfully for other clients and will work successfully in this situation, too.

The information about pro bono projects on this resumé also provides useful, if more subtle, information to potential clients. The Editorial Freelancers Association (EFA) activity indicates that this person is committed to freelancing. Both the EFA and Women in Toys activities suggest that she is connected to networks of other professionals. To a potential client, this means she's serious about her career and may be able to recommend others for any work she can't do herself—a useful attribute in a freelancer.

The functional resumé concludes with a traditional academic degree statement. This is also the place to list other relevant qualifications, such as a Board of Editors in the Life Sciences (BELS) certification or a certificate from another respected program (such as those offered by the University of California San Diego Extension, the University of Chicago Graham School, or the Poynter Institute). Courses from the EFA, ACES: The Society for Editing, and other professional organizations are also valuable. While clients may prefer to see practical experience, completing courses and earning certificates from recognized sources shows that you're committed to lifelong learning and professional development. They can also be useful if you don't have a lot of work experience.

Figure 3 is another excellent example of a functional resumé. Like Figure 2, this resumé also has an eye-catching heading that characterizes this person as a serious professional freelancer. The overall design is contemporary, clean, and easy to read. The Summary offers a clear, focused explanation of this person's skills and services and shows that this freelancer is aware of current resumé trends by omitting the traditional Objective statement, which is no longer considered necessary. The Selected Clients list that follows is impressive, and the Highlights section is a creative and efficient way to present skills.

MARY RATCLIFFE CORPORATE COMMUNICATIONS

304 West 75th Street, New York, NY 10023
Maryratcliffe@hmail.com, 212-787-1234, maryratcliffe.com

SUMMARY	Versatile writer/editor/designer experienced in the creation and production of brochures, newsletters, product collaterals, news releases, sales promotion pieces, advertising copy, website content, and corporate speeches. Easy-to-read prose that demystifies industry-specific jargon and makes technical information accessible to lay readers.
SKILLS & ABILITIES	Highly skilled graphic designer with expertise in InDesign, PowerPoint, Photoshop, digital photography. Award-winning advertising writer.
SELECTED CLIENTS	Takeda USA/Takeda Chemical Industries Thoroughbred Retirement Foundation (TRF) Macmillan Publishing Koehler Iversen, Inc. Lee Nordstrom Galleries Gale Research
HIGHLIGHTS	Product collaterals support $250 million in annual sales for Takeda USA. Speeches for Takeda top executives include keynote addresses at international symposia and conferences. TRF fundraising newsletter has raised as much as $26,000 with a single issue. B2B ads have been ranked in top percentiles by independent recognition/recall studies. News releases for clients are carried by trade and consumer press. Artists' exhibition catalogs are preserved in Archives of American Art.

Figure 3. Functional resumé.

Eleanor Editor
Street Address
City, State ZIPcode
Phone, 123-456-7890
E-mail, Eleanor@aol.com

SUMMARY: Researcher, Editor, Copyeditor, writer of legal, technical, advocacy, community outreach papers. Lawyer in private practice in Washington, D.C. Legislative and policy analysis.

EXPERIENCE:

1991-94: **Researcher, copyeditor,** *On Prejudice: A Global Perspective* (Anchor Doubleday, N.Y.). Author/editor Daniela Gioseffi, P.O. Box 15, Andover, NJ 07821 (201) 786-7947.

1991-95: **Editor,** *Investment proposals, reviews of project financing, mergers and acquisitions,* Bayard Group, LTD, Anthony J. Scarola, Partner, Box 51, Blairstown, NJ 07825 (908) 362-5310.

1992-95: **Copyeditor,** *scientific and industrial reports for Ph.D. Consultant in Industrial Chemistry,* Dr. Lionel B. Luttinger, Drew Chemical Corp. Research and Development, One Drew Plaza, Boonton, NJ 07005. Home address: 24 Glen Cove Rd., Andover, NJ 07821 (201) 263-7600/(201)786-7947.

1984-91: **Editor, writer, researcher,** *Institute for Advanced Research in Asian Science and Medicine.* Co-authored, edited, researched reports and papers on Asian medicine. Frederick Kao, M.D. (deceased) and John Kao, M.D., Editor, *Journal of IARASM,* P.O. Box 67336, Chestnut Hill, MA 02167.

1989-95: **Researcher, writer, editor, organizer:** *Paulinskill-Pequest Watershed Assoc., Inc.,* served as Chair Executive Committee; currently member Board of Trustees; wrote legal papers for incorporation; researched and wrote advocacy papers; researched, wrote and edited testimony to municipal and regional governments. Ursula Perrin, 26 East Crisman Rd., Blairstown, NJ 07825. Editor, *Currents* (newsletter) (908) 362-9125.

1987-89: **Writer, researcher,** *Companion; Warren County Magazine,* Editor, Proprietor, Paul Avery, Cabbages & Kings Book Store, Blairstown, NJ 07825 (908) 362-5142.

1977-86: **FORMERLY: Attorney in Private Practice, Washington, D.C.**

Represented Asian Health Association of Metropolitan Washington. Wrote and researched testimony before Maryland Department of Health and Maryland legislature, liaised with membership-government. Was instrumental in achieving legalization, licensing and regulation for Asian medical practices. Dr. Ralph Coan, 4400 East-West Highway, Bethesda, Maryland 20016. Personal commendation from Dept. of Labor for research and testimony that established new federal-level standard of training and experience for Asian health practitioners.

Assistant Director, Washington Office, Amnesty International USA and previously, as Legal Intern: In-depth research and analysis of U.S. refugee policy. Wrote recommendations adopted by Executive Committee. Managed government relations efforts and directed reform of refugee laws; developed and maintained contact with key members of Congress. Consultant for Ford Foundation project: Wrote, researched and developed survey exploring data on human rights which created international human rights database used by Amnesty International and other groups.

Teacher of English for a variety of Japanese companies, Hiroshima, Japan.

EDUCATION:

J.D. Columbus School of Law, C.U.A., Washington, D.C.
B.A. The George Washington University, Washington, D.C.

Figure 4. This traditional resumé follows the reverse chronological format. The email at the top of the page is from an aol .com account. The experience section is cluttered with addresses and telephone numbers of former employers.

Creating Your
Functional Resumé

Even if you're new to freelancing, you should be able to create a solid functional resumé by rethinking your traditional one. Be creative without stretching the truth. Look at the skills you used in all the jobs you've had, including those outside publishing. And remember: skills developed through volunteer work (your co-op's newsletter, for example) also count.

For an example of how a traditional resumé can be converted into a functional resumé, compare Figures 4 and 5.

Figure 4, a traditional resumé, is more confusing than helpful to a potential client. The Summary suggests that the applicant is seeking either editorial or legal work, while the chronological approach presents a jumble of skills applied in a variety of overlapping and part-time jobs, mostly outside traditional publishing.

Figure 5, a functional resumé, extracts the valuable skills hidden in the traditional resumé and highlights them in a way that emphasizes writing and editorial skills for specific clients. The real-life freelancer who provided these examples (who preferred to remain anonymous) experienced a sizable increase in business when she began sending out the functional version.

Figure 4 follows the reverse chronological format. The email address at the top of the page is from a generic, and unprofessional, aol.com account. The Experience section is cluttered with unneeded addresses and telephone numbers of former employers.

Figure 5, a skills-based resumé, features an email address and a website URL that reflect the freelancer's professionalism. The resumé offers a clear portrait of the freelancer by summarizing experience, highlighting valued clients, and emphasizing career achievements, eliminating the clutter found in Figure 4.

Figures 6 and 7 also illustrate the impact of recasting a traditional resumé into a functional one.

Eleanor Editor
Street Address
City, State ZIPcode
123-456-7890
Owner@EleanorEditor.com, www.EleanorEditor.com

SUMMARY

Copyeditor, line editor, writer, research-analyst with experience in law and legislation, Chinese and Japanese history and culture, healthcare reform issues, the environment, and literature. Experience in editing book manuscripts, legislative testimony, position papers, speeches, business communications. Specialize in editing legal, scholarly, high-quality literary materials; polishing work of non-native speakers.

SELECTED CLIENTS

Institute for Advanced Research in Asian Science and Medicine (publishes books, journals)
William Morrow & Company, Inc., Adult Trade Books Division
Amnesty International USA (human rights organization)
Warren County magazine
Bayard Group, Ltd. (joint ventures, investment financing)
Journal of New Jersey Poets
Star-Ledger newspaper
Ford Foundation

HIGHLIGHTS

- Wrote position paper analyzing U.S. laws that became basis of Amnesty International USA's refugee policy.
- Co-authored UNESCO journal article; researched and wrote articles, papers, about Asian medicine in America.
- Responsible for proofreading and slugging of all adult trade books and flap copy for William Morrow.
- Researched and wrote standard reference work for *Journal of Health Politics, Policy, and Law* about regulation of Asian medical practices in the U.S.
- Edited section of biography of former head of Department of Biology, Yenching (now Beijing) University, China.
- Researched and wrote legislative testimony instrumental in achieving licensing of Asian medical practices; drafted Washington, D.C., statute.
- Proposed and developed series of articles on land use and municipal government for regional magazine.
- Designed and wrote brochure for largest Asian medical clinic on the East Coast; wrote all business materials.

HONORS AND AWARDS

- Personal commendation from U.S. Department of Labor for research and testimony establishing new federal-level standards for training and experience of Asian medical practitioners.
- First prize in Stewart Stiller Writing Competition for work of fiction based on analysis of Chinese criminal code.

PRO BONO

- Research, write, edit advocacy papers, legislative testimony for Paulinskill-Pequest Watershed Association.

EDUCATION

- BA, George Washington University
- JD, Columbus School of Law, Catholic University of America
- Editing courses, Publishing Institute, New York University.

Figure 5. This skills-based resumé presents an email address that reflects the professionalism of the freelancer, and the website URL emphasizes this. The resumé presents a strong portrait of the freelancer by summarizing experience, highlighting valued diverse clients, and emphasizing career achievements, eliminating the clutter found in Figure 4.

Fred Freelancer

Street Address
City, State ZIPcode
Email address
Phone number
Website URL

Figure 6. Traditional resumé.

Freelance Technical Editor

SUMMARY:
- Strong English language skills
- Broad knowledge of the natural sciences
- Published researcher
- MS in Environmental Microbiology

EXPERIENCE:
Freelance Technical Editor (July 2015–Present)
Edit research papers, grant proposals, books, and presentations. Correct language errors and improve the clarity, organization, readability, and logical flow of manuscripts. Provide authors with constructive feedback. Format documents to meet journal or agency specifications.
- Cambridge University Press (**Agriculture**)
- Chinese Academy of Sciences (**Microbiome**)
- Wordvice (**Environmental Microbiology**)
- University of Massachusetts (**Environmental Engineering, chemistry**)
- Mount Holyoke College (**Ecology**)
- Worcester Polytechnic Institute (**Chemical Engineering**)
- Amherst College (**Biology**)
- University of Gothenburg (**Marine Sciences**)
- Editage (**Toxicology**)

Science and Technology Educator (2004–2015)
Generated excitement for STEM topics in K–12 students by developing hands-on workshops in pond water life, microscopy, Lego robotics, science fair projects, and math. Coached middle school robotics teams.

Scientist (1997–1999)
Planned, carried out, and published research on bioremediation of marine sediment as a civilian contractor to the Space and Naval Warfare Systems Command facility in San Diego.

PUBLICATIONS:
Freelancer, F.F. & Crowley, D.E. (2001). Duration of lag phase of *Pseudomonas fluorescens* 2-79RL starved in isolation or in the presence of soil microorganisms. *Soil Biology and Biochemistry, 33,* 2005–2010.

Apitz, S.E., Arias, E., Clawson, S.A., **Freelancer, F.F.**, Melcher, R.J., & Hemmingsen, B.B. (1999). The development of a sterile, PAH-spiked, aged marine sediment for biodegrad… *Organic Geochemistry, 30,* 891–900.

EDUCATION:
MS, Environmental Microbiology, Ur…
BA, Journalism, University of Massa…

Fred Freelancer

Street Address
City, State ZIPcode
Email address
Phone number
Website URL

Freelance Technical Editor

SUMMARY:
- Specialist in medical and natural sciences editing
- Fluent in AMA and CSE style
- Editorial expertise with research manuscripts, monographs, white papers, grant proposals, abstracts, proposals, slide decks, and educational content
- Board of Editors in the Life Sciences (BELS) certification
- MS in Environmental Microbiology
- Published researcher

EXPERIENCE:
Edit research papers, grant proposals, books, presentations, and other materials. Correct language errors and improve the clarity, organization, readability, and logical flow of manuscripts. Provide authors with constructive feedback. Format documents to meet journal or agency specifications.

AREAS OF EXPERTISE
Extensive knowledge and experience with clinical trials, medicine, biology, microbiology, biochemistry, genetics, oncology, pharmacology, toxicology, infectious diseases, food science, environmental science, and biotechnology.

RECENT CLIENTS
- Cambridge University Press
- Chinese Academy of Sciences
- Wordvice
- Tufts Medical Center
- American Association of Critical-Care Nurses
- Cactus Communications/Editage

PUBLICATIONS:
Freelancer, F. & Crowley, D.E. (2001). Duration of lag phase of *Pseudomonas fluorescens* 2-79RL starved in isolation or in the presence of soil microorganisms. *Soil Biology and Biochemistry, 33,* 2005–2010.

Apitz, S.E., Arias, E., Clawson, S.A., Freelancer, F., Melcher, R.J., & Hemmingsen, B.B. (1999). The development of a sterile, PAH-spiked, aged marine sediment for biodegradation experiments: Chemical results. *Organic Geochemistry, 30,* 891–900.

EDUCATION:
MS, Environmental Microbiology, University of California Riverside

BA, Journalism, University of Massachusetts Amherst

Figure 7. Functional resumé.

Designing Your Functional Resumé

The appearance of your resumé makes a difference — it should be simply but attractively designed. Remember that the principal purpose is to convey information effectively, so don't overdo the design elements. Use no more than two fonts or typefaces and select common ones that are easy to read. Avoid using color (in the text or as a design element), boxes or lines, and similar decorative items. You don't know what device your prospective client will use to view or print your resumé, and it may end up being scanned or viewed on a small phone screen, so the less fussy, the better. For emailed resumés, make sure all hyperlinks are functional. For mailing on paper, although that's increasingly rare, it should be printed on high-quality letterhead.

Rather than struggling to come up with an attractive design on your own, search the web for resumé templates — you'll find many, many options. Choose one that's simple and easy to update.

A good resumé is concise, so don't waste precious space with a photo. Not only can you use that area to present more of your skills and experience, but a headshot may also confuse automated systems that can't cope with design aspects like those of the resumé in Figure 8. Even more significant, the photo can result in discrimination, whether conscious or not. An otherwise acceptable resumé may be tossed because of technological issues — or implicit bias.

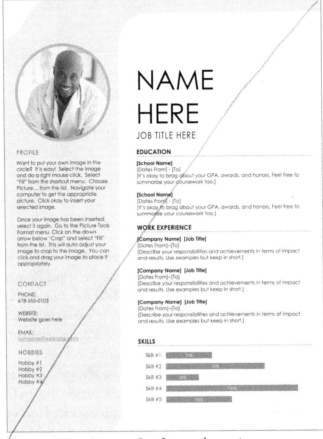

Figure 8. Overformatted resumé.

Figure 8 shows an overformatted resumé.

Today, hiring and human resources professionals often use artificial intelligence (AI) or algorithms to assess and filter resumés. AI apps use natural-language processing, search engine optimization (SEO), and keywords to sift through resumés and score them according to a candidate's suitability for a job. That means you have to include key terms from a project description for your skills to be noticed and relayed to the prospective client. If the key terms in a job description aren't already in your resumé, add them as needed—and be sure they're in your cover letter. Some apps also only recognize certain typefaces or fonts, which is yet another reason to be conservative with design. You're more likely to encounter AI apps or algorithms when applying for a full-time job, but these types of automation may also affect how your freelance resumé is treated.

As you become established as a freelancer, you may find that you send out fewer resumés because more of your work comes from repeat clients and direct referrals. It's still important to review and update your resumé periodically, however. If you don't, there will inevitably come the day when you want to immediately send your resumé to an exciting potential client who requests it, only to realize that it's two years out of date and you need more time than you have to get it up to speed.

One other advantage of a functional resumé is that a client is more likely to be impressed by it and keep it on file than a traditional chronological one. You may not be offered an immediate assignment, but you may improve your chances of being contacted in the future.

Sending Out
Your Resumé

When you're ready to send out your resumé, pay attention to any requirements or guidelines in a listing. If a potential client says they won't accept attachments, copy and paste your resumé into the email and provide links to any other material.

As you set up or update your resumé, be sure to label it in a distinct way. Name the file something like YourNameResumé.docx or .pdf, not just resumé.docx, so it's easily identifiable if it gets separated from your email or cover letter. This will also make it stand out from submissions by other freelancers.

Many successful freelancers have several functional resumés that are distinct from one another and tailored to different potential clients. Once you've completed a basic functional resumé, you can design a job-specific version for each submission or at least craft a separate, targeted cover letter for each.

Cover letters remain vital to interacting with prospective clients. Your resumé provides information about your background; the cover letter can be tailored to each opportunity. If you prefer to have only one version of your resumé, a cover letter can show how your skills and experience meet that specific client's needs.

As with traditional job hunting, your cover letter offers a chance to stand out and explain why you're a good match for a project or assignment. This is where you want to be assertive and self-promotional.

It's also where more self-effacing or introverted editorial freelancers have difficulty. You are an accomplished professional—let your skills and personality shine.

Supplementing Your Resumé

A resumé often isn't enough. This is particularly true for big projects where the client must be persuaded that your skills are the right ones, but it's also a factor of today's online world. You may want to send the client additional information such as publication or project lists, writing or editing samples, and letters of reference or testimonials. You also need to have a presence on networks like LinkedIn, which is where many potential clients go to find freelance professionals with editorial skills.

A LinkedIn profile can be detailed and deep, with much the same information as a resumé, and without the classic two-page limit. Be sure to pull as much relevant information from your resumé into your LinkedIn profile as possible, and look for ways to enhance that profile to make yourself stand out. A strong LinkedIn profile is another way to show prospective clients how you can meet their needs.

For a guide to using LinkedIn effectively, EFA member Chris Morton, an expert in this area, recommends Wayne Breitbarth's book The Power Formula for LinkedIn Success. (Be sure to use the most recent edition, as it's updated regularly.)

These days, it's important, if not vital, to support your resumé with a website (or vice versa!) that provides further background about who you are and what you do. Think of a website as a greatly expanded, in-depth version of your resumé, as well as your portfolio. This is where you can show more detail through your work samples, testimonials, publication lists, client lists, awards, certifications, and other accomplishments. You can even include a blog that potential clients can subscribe to, thus building your email list of leads to nurture with more content and special offers.

You can also support your resumé through your social media profiles by sharing your blog posts, links, photos, and commentary. Potential clients will almost certainly check you out on social media, including your personal profiles if you allow open access to them, so be cautious about what you post publicly and be selective about who can see your personal posts. Photos of you accepting an award or speaking at a conference, yes. Photos of you well into the post-conference happy hour, no.

Surprisingly, many editorial freelancers don't keep up-to-date lists of their clients and completed projects, even though such a list is an effective marketing tool and should be part of your resumé, website, and LinkedIn profile. The information in this master list should be detailed and include the skill used (e.g., copyediting), client name, project title, and date. Direct potential clients to the full list or send one tailored to the particular assignment you're interested in.

Freelancers treasure the rare letter of thanks for a job well done. There's nothing immodest about posting testimonials on social media or sharing them with a possible client, or requesting a testimonial or reference letter from a satisfied client. You can ask clients for recommendations on LinkedIn, request testimonials via email, or create a brief survey to send to clients after their project is complete; many online resources offer free survey options. Be sure to include a testimonials page on your website.

Clients sometimes ask for samples of past editorial work. This request is often impossible for copyeditors or proofreaders to accommodate, as some work is proprietary and many clients don't want anyone to see the "before" versions of their projects. Tactfully explain that you can't provide samples for ethical reasons, and direct them to your client or project list, testimonials or reference letters, and your resumé. If you really want the work, offer to take a short proofreading or copyediting test, or to edit or proofread a short sample of the project. You can also ask past or existing clients if you can share segments of their marked-up documents anonymously, but never do so without written permission.

Most writers and journalists supplement a resumé with running lists, in reverse chronological order, of their published books, articles, and other projects, along with cover images, links, and downloadable excerpts of their work. A publications list should include the full title, periodical or publisher, date of publication, and some brief details (e.g., awards or sales figures). Many writers also keep copies of favorable reviews to send along with a project list.

Writing samples can be a problem, particularly if you're trying to break into a new area. Try to send only recent, relevant examples; never send fiction, poetry, or other creative writing. Provide PDFs or links to samples — don't send originals on paper, because they won't be returned.

Alternatives to Resumés

Freelancers are so accustomed to being asked for, and providing, resumés that they rarely question the point of the exercise. But do you really need a resumé? Other professionals who provide services (accountants, for example) may send resumés to prospective clients, but they also have business cards, brochures, and other promotional materials, as well as a website, LinkedIn profile, and other ways of marketing themselves and their work. These make a good, businesslike impression, proving that they are confident professionals.

Freelancers should also carry attractive, quality business cards. Inexpensive and convenient, a business card is an effective marketing tool. It should include your name, contact information, website URL, and your logo or any other identifying artwork that you use on your resumé and website. Give them to friends, colleagues, clients, and potential clients. Where resumés get deleted or thrown away, cards are kept, sometimes to be retrieved and used long after you handed them out.

A brief, well-produced brochure outlining your services and credentials is another effective alternative to a resumé. It may be the preferred approach if you're dealing with clients outside the publishing world—to them, you're just one more service provider. A brochure offers more opportunities for snappy copy, but it's also more complex to think through and produce. Although the ins and outs of producing the text of a good brochure are too detailed to go into here, free or inexpensive brochure templates are easy to find online. Print your brochure using a high-quality color printer or a reputable print shop, mail copies to prospective clients, and hand them out at meetings and conferences.

Targeting Your Resumé

Once you've developed your functional resumé, created your LinkedIn profile, and gotten some business cards, the next step is to get them to the right people. Who are the right people? Anyone who has the power to assign editorial work. Unless you're working directly with independent authors, freelance work is generally assigned by middle-level staffers: managing editors, copy chiefs, production editors, associate editors, and others with similar titles. Target your marketing to them. If you send your resumé to editorial directors or publishers, they (or their assistants) may be more likely to delete it than pass it on.

Titles and functions vary from one company to another, so you may have to ask around a bit or search the company's website to find the right person. Look up the company online to learn not only what it does but also who does what and how to contact them. Publication and company websites often provide submission guidelines for freelancers, as well as editorial calendars so you can tailor your pitch and resumé to their needs. Network with your professional colleagues—it's okay to ask if anyone knows the appropriate contact at Company X or Publication Y.

Once you figure out who assigns the work, send that person a resumé with a short cover letter and a link to your website, LinkedIn profile, or other online portfolio. If you're using paper, print your resumé on letterhead stationery and attach a business card. Follow up by email a week or two later. If no work is available at the moment and the person tells you to check back in a month or so, do that. If they don't suggest checking back, ask when a good time would be, but keep it low-key; don't be pushy.

Even if the client seems reluctant, follow up. If no work or possible date for future work is forthcoming during this second follow-up, stop for now and try again in a few months. Remember that the need for freelancers ebbs and flows within a company; a resumé sent today may result in work many months later.

When responding to online job postings (through the EFA Job List, for example), apply only if you're well qualified. Tailor your resumé and cover letter to the opportunity, highlighting how you match the requested skills and experience. Research the client online and write a short, targeted cover letter to accompany the resumé. Include relevant samples and links. Act promptly—online job posts draw a heavy response. Get your resumé in quickly with a cover letter that makes you stand out.

Your resumé can help freelance work come to you. Most professional organizations have job-filling resources for clients. The EFA, for example, has an online, searchable directory that clients use to find freelancers—a strong profile there is likely to bring projects to you, as potential clients will see your resumé and other information you post there. This is preferable to looking for clients or competing with dozens to hundreds of colleagues for opportunities posted through organizational job lists or on job search engines. Be sure to review your profiles periodically to keep them up to date.

Words of Warning

Sadly, the world of job hunting is full of scammers. Some have figured out how to pull names and email addresses from organizational membership directories and use them to their own benefit. If you get an offer that seems too good to be true, it probably is.

The overpayment scam is the most common. If you respond to a message about an unsolicited freelance project and the "client" sends you a check for more than the amount discussed, be very cautious. Call the bank on the check to make sure it's legitimate. If you deposit it into your account, the sender is likely to write back that they accidentally sent you more than requested and ask you to return the "difference." Once you do that, the "client" will disappear and you'll be out the amount you sent them, the total of the deposited fraudulent check, and any fees that result from using the money they sent you. Depending on your state's criminal defense laws, you could even be held responsible for depositing a fake check.

Another common scam involves an email message saying that a company found you through one of your professional memberships. They're offering work outside your usual field and want to interview you using Google Hangouts. Run!

If you have questions about a client or payment, belonging to an organization like the EFA comes in handy. Ask your colleagues about any project offer that seems iffy.

And finally, be prepared. You may not get a response to some of your pitches or replies to job listings. This is discouraging but normal; it can take a while to build a steady client base. Don't give up—craft or polish that resumé and keep at it!

Suggested Reading

Libraries and bookstores are full of books with titles about how to write a winning or effective resumé, although these tend to be oriented toward readers looking for full-time work in traditional settings. Freelancers seeking advice about resumés may find books on changing careers, marketing, and entrepreneurship more helpful. The internet teems with advice from reliable and successful experts as well, from blog posts to websites and videos.

One classic that remains useful is the most recent edition of *What Color Is Your Parachute?* by Richard N. Bolles. To plug in to current trends and techniques, browse the shelves at your neighborhood library or bookstore for newer offerings, and search the internet for tips and examples.

About the Authors

 Sheila Buff is a bestselling writer, coauthor, and ghostwriter specializing in health, nutrition, and consumer-oriented medicine who has been a freelancer since 1981. A longtime EFA member, she served as coexecutive director from 1995 to 2001, founded the EFA Discussion List, serves as Job List chairperson, and wrote the original version of this booklet.

 **Ruth E. Thaler-Carter** is an award-winning freelance writer, editor, proofreader, desktop publisher, and speaker whose motto is "I can write about anything!"® She is the editor of the EFA's bimonthly newsletter; coordinator of the St. Louis chapter and past coordinator of the Rochester, New York, chapter; author of *Freelancing 101: Launching Your Editorial Business* for the EFA; chairperson of the EFA's 2005 national conference and speaker at its 2013 and 2019 conferences; and a frequent presenter of workshops, webinars, and conference sessions for the EFA and other organizations. She is also the creator of Communication Central's annual Be a Better Freelancer® conference; owner of the publishing company A Flair for Writing and the blog *An American Editor*; and Networking Expert for the National Association of Independent Writers and Editors (NAIWE).

EMPOWERING EDITORIAL
FREELANCERS SINCE 1970

About the
Editorial Freelancers Association (EFA)

Celebrating 50 Years!
Dedicated to the Education and Growth
of Editorial Freelancers

The EFA is a national not-for-profit — 501(c)6 — organization, headquartered in New York City, run by member volunteers, all of whom are also freelancers. The EFA's members, experienced in a wide range of professional skills, live and work all across the United States and in other countries.

A pioneer in organizing freelancers into a network for mutual support and advancement, the EFA is now recognized throughout the publishing industry as the source for professional editorial assistance.

We welcome people of every race, color, culture, religion or no religion, gender identity, gender expression, age, national or ethnic origin, ancestry, citizenship, education, ability, health, neurotype, marital/parental status, socio-economic background, sexual orientation, and/or military status. We are nothing without our members, and encourage everyone to volunteer and to participate in our community.

The EFA sells a variety of specialized booklets, not unlike this one, on topics of interest to editorial freelancers at the-efa.org.

The EFA hosts online, asynchronous courses, real-time webinars, and on-demand recorded webinars designed especially for freelance editors, writers, and other editorial specialists around the world. You can learn more about our Education Program at the-efa.org.

To learn about these and other EFA offerings, visit the-efa.org and join us on social media:

Twitter: @EFAFreelancers
Instagram: @efa_editors
Facebook: editorialfreelancersassociation
LinkedIn: editorial-freelancers

CPSIA information can be obtained
at www.ICGtesting.com
Printed in the USA
BVHW040854030121
596865BV00049B/2547